Back to Alabama

Sundress Publications • Knoxville, TN

Editor: Sherrel McLafferty
Managing Editor: Tennison Black
Editorial Assistant: Kanika Lawton
Editorial Interns: Whitney Cooper, Caitlin Mulqueen, Zora Satchell, and K Slade

Colophon: This book is set in Noto Serif
Cover Art: "Calliope" by Willie Schofield
Cover Design: Kristen Ton
Book Design: Sherrel McLafferty

Back to Alabama
Valerie A. Smith

Acknowledgements

Many thanks to the editors and staff of the following publications in which these poems first appeared.

Ariel Chart: "First Sunday in November"
Auburn Avenue: "Legion: For We Are Many," "Winter in Georgia,"
  and "Back to Alabama"
Aunt Chloe: A Journal of Artful Candor: "Unreliable Narrator" and
  "Miles Davis: The Horn, The Iris, and The Sorcerer"
Bellingham Review: "15 reasons why you mad Brittney Griner is free"
BlazeVox: "The Man in Our Family Portrait" and "To Function or
  Operate Properly"
Call + Response: "Burn the whole thing" and "Alice Walker's 75th
  Birthday Celebration, Eatonton, Georgia"
The Crambo: "The Spare Bedroom"
Crosswinds Poetry Journal: "Weep with Those Who Weep"
Dogwood: A Journal of Poetry and Prose: "Harriet Tubman as a
Caseworker" and "On the Death of Chadwick Boseman"
Exit 271: Your Georgia Writers Resource: "Moon Rising" and
  "The Ocean"
Hoxie Gorge Review: "The Cost of Living"
Obsidian: "The Other Nine," "Threshing Floor," and "Return"
Oyster River Pages: "Holy City: Charleston, SC"
Shō Poetry Journal: "Curlie Raised the Blues" and "Carol 'Money'
  Blue married in"
Solstice Literary Journal: "Expert of the Apricot Groves"
South Carolina Review: "Application for Angels" and "Queen & Slim"
South85: "Curlie Blue"
Typehouse Literary Magazine: "The Sugar Shack" and "These are
  the rules on your weekend home from the psych ward"
Wayne Literary Review: "Black Don't Crack and Other Tales in
  Multiple Choice"
Weber—The Contemporary West: "Curlie Raised the Blues," and "Rain
  on a September Morning"

Contents

Return

If I go to Africa
it will seep into my skin,
the dirt, I mean, the sound
dirt makes when it's birthing,
all breathy, heavy, and rising.
I'll inhale the incense by accident
and hear my heart beat.

If I go to Africa
I'll catch fire like a briar bush.
The sun will burn me into the sand,
wash me down a great river
and over an even greater fall.
I'll become loud if I go to Africa.
Screaming, screaming loud.

I can hear it now,
the sand, I mean, lifting into the wind,
brushing the trees. I will stand
in the middle of Africa,
in the middle of the world,
and let its wholeness swallow me,
fold over me like a paper coffin.

A blanket, I mean.
There is so little between death
and sleep. I'll live in that rest if I go.
I won't want to go anywhere else.
There will be no leaving, nowhere
the voice sounds like bone and fruit,
sweet, crunchy, and soft.

I can taste Africa sometimes
in my own mouth. It rises like
daybreak and makes me blush.
I remember what I've never seen.
I'm only guessing. Africa, I mean,

the sand, covering, spreading, tastes
like where the rain meets the sky.

I.

Back to Alabama

No one wants to go back to fall in love
with rebellion. She is a debutante
dressed in white. She has plans to keep
her man in Alabama; no matter how
he comes. It's always from the North

through Chattanooga or from the East
over the Appalachians, a monster sleeping
on its side, elbow up in New Hampshire,
hips sloped at Kentucky, bumpy thighs and
knees knotty all the way to Birmingham.

No one wants to ride that dragon again, not even
for a wife and two children: pride and reparation.
Debutante is going to have to find her way back
by herself, back home where tornadoes play
hop-scotch on the soft side of Monte Sano.

The kids grow like weeds. They defy all odds.
They have no rebellion. They have no plans
for reconstruction. They float around like hoverflies
in the mountain valley breeze. At dusk, they wander
towards the light, and here we go back to Alabama

where great grandfather's farm is grown over
to a ramshackle color of possum fur, a shadow
leaning in the evergreen. Where headstones sink
in moss, covered with broken pecan shells,
the fresh ones and the rotten ones, black as soot.

Curlie Blue

The Blues down south would cut you
like a paper mill and let your rotten stink
blow all the way north on a hot summer
breeze. That's how she left, you know.

She was the second oldest of thirteen,
stocky as a sawed-off shotgun, red hair,
freckles and plump green eyes that traced
an un-retraceable line.

When I met her, she was Sunday dressed
in a full-length cashmere coat and matching
camel-colored hat. The wide brim over
her right eye leaned into each heavy stride.

Legend has it, she snatched a black snake
out an oak tree in mid conversation and
ripped his head off in the street. She gripped
my hand and pulled a knife one night–

we stayed too late at Menlo Park Mall
and had to walk out the service exit.
I was just tall enough to see the blade
flash in the corner of my eye.

Her anointed hands could rub a rash clean
and make me believe the Blues
were always one bitter snuff can away
from spittin' out the truth.

Holy City: Charleston, SC

I was once free to give and let live until the tides turned
ship after ship against my shores, ripping my sandy skirt and
shredding me like blades of Bermuda.

This womb survived like a twin grabbing his brother's ankle,
fighting for birthright over a bowl of she-crab soup.
I never said welcome when they entered spilling souls.

Militant is my middle name for battling malaria
against the massas and the missuses. Grandmothers
used to call me a haint, and here lies Princess Xualla.

You say I am your favorite place to visit, and I laugh
because I'm in your feet standing on my shoulders.
I'm in a hundred thousand pairs of daylight eyes.

Spend the weekend wading through my bones. My bosom
gleams moist with milk. My babies, snake-bitten, drowned
by Ashley & Cooper. Listen to the wind weeping.

Welcome, and we become each other's suicide pact:
I'll die if you die. That's what he must have said
when he cut Christ down at Mother Emmanuel.

I serve a meal so rich in blood you might become a cannibal.
So fed up with the change of my complexion, I can't afford
to look you in the mirror. Return to Folly.

My blueprint reads like Smalls and Equiano calling
from the earth. Four hundred years later, and I
am the closest you'll ever get back to Africa.

Curlie Raised the Blues

in a North Jersey brownstone,
its cellar door alarmed with tin cans.
Her blue china shined on impeccable taste.

She was there baking fresh biscuits and gravy
when the Blues escaped the South
on busses and trains. Her home

became a depot for young siblings
to be raised with her only son.
She taught him to read and

never laid a hand on him.
She put her brothers on big rigs
and married her sisters to affable men.

Me and all my second cousins
swam in her above-ground pool,
ate watermelon at the picnic table
kicking pincher bugs off our toes.

When I lost hold of her dog
and chased him around the city block,
she sent me to the yard for a switch
but she couldn't bear to use it.

She'd rather lick her thumb
and catch the Bible's thin pages
with a shotgun under her bed
and Harlequins in the attic.

"Black Don't Crack" and Other Tales in Multiple Choice

1. She runs to my lap and screams,
    a. I love my hair and all my friends want to touch it.
    b. I love my hair!
    c. yellow
    d. nothing. I pull her back into my womb and show her copper.

2. You have beautiful skin. To which I reply,
    a. My mother has skin like milk chocolate.
    b. Thank you.
    c. Soap and water.
    d. This poem's title.

3. You will be the only one going to jail out of a room full of people all holding the same
    a. weight
    b. body
    c. metal
    d. breath

4. Magical Negro: Because these are our rules, you cannot use someone else's
    a. comb
    b. brush
    c. makeup
    d. man

5. He shoulders to my shoulder and asks when he will grow a mustache, and I say,
    a. Your father's grandmother was Ute.
    b. Your mother's grandmother was Cherokee.
    c. Your uncle's mustache just came in. He's 46.
    d. nothing, thinking about so many people.

6. History
    a. He worked on the railroad.
    b. He worked on the railroad.
    c. He worked on the railroad.
    d. He worked on the railroad.

7. Your cousin is
    a. Jesse Owens
    b. John Stallworth
    c. a neuroscientist
    d. waiting for you

Carol "Money" Blue married in

through Curlie's youngest brother,
the twin of a dead boy. Their love
burned hot and cold at the same time.

When I met her, she was at the door
in eyeballs and bones, her face a glowing
skeleton, her hips a lantern in gauchos,
her voice a high hollow of familiar.

I was just old enough to answer, to crack
the door open and keep her out, to steel
my breath at death staring me to wonder,
if she looked like this,

then what about my uncle?
Where were my cousins?
A block away, laminate peeled off
the edge of the table like an onion.

No one recovered, though she sobered
years later, her face permanently misshapen,
and handed us—the bride and groom—
a Kool cigarette in a glass case.

Threshing Floor
High Museum of Art, African Art Collection

A grass-woven threshing basket
old as the colonies and black as a swamp bog,
rested round and flat, four feet in diameter,
on a square white platform.

I imagined her two hundred years ago,
testing its concentric flexibility. I wondered
if my arms could reach around.

She gripped its sides,
held the body against her body,
and lifted, tossed the grass high.

Tiny grains of rice ran toward her belly,
separated into place and found the grooves,
circles marked by crescents where they met.

As the chaff rose to the sky
she heard *Creator*.
As the chaff rose to the sky
she heard *Creator of the Universe*.

Expert of the Apricot Groves

She comes bearing fruit,
rock-serious ovaries birth
without breaking, bloom white
as winter leaves overnight.

She comes bearing fruit,
finger-circled gifts settle
into levels, reduce swelling,
the heart of a late summer.

She never studied history,
or faraway. Dirt yields, joy
blossoms wherever she says,
If it grows, it grows.

She sees my fallow garden
as proof of possibility. *There,
there,* and points to harvests
I can't see.

She comes bearing fruit, asks
Do you like apricots? I don't
answer. I open to be cured,
recover, plant a seed.

Harriet Tubman as a Caseworker

These nights, no one is home.
Caseloads of young,
the North Star, foggy.

When I was a child
someone hit me so hard
I lost my sense of beauty.

I hear the ocean beating
where the ice marches
over the shore. Freedom

is the choice to cross
a river, tell a child
another world exists.

I am not the only one.
If you look out at night
you'll hear them calling.

Alice Walker's 75th Birthday Celebration, Eatonton, Georgia

First, quiet
determination.
A body takes
less space
than a body
needs: knees
stacked neatly,
thighs so close
they equaled
one of mine.

Then, what air
couldn't weigh
sat frozen under
a black wig. Our
tears dropped
an arm rest
apart.

I wanted to say, *Honey,*
we are all
visible
here.
She has taught us
to fly.

II.

"The Sugar Shack"
    Ernie Barnes, 1971

Ernie says, Eyes closed.

Feel this funky bass bottom blue
Big Daddy Rucker on that sway belly sax
Two-Hands Trumpet blowin the air out this joint
Preacher Man got the spirit leaned back on the mic
Ol' Pop Porter sittin by his bottle thinkin on ways
He used to grab them gals by the hips   same old news

Sophisticated White Dress sings the blues
Lean in Red Dress lean out breathe
Denim Slacks Derby Hat moan and groan
Not one square foot without an upturned foot
Not one plankboard without a pump
All this brown skin moving brown fingers feeling
All this   electric   light   shining

Bald heads, says Ernie.
Let us be   thinking   skeletal
                human   heads high
Let us be   open&   close-mouthed
                ecstasy   &existential
Let us be   bountiful   doubleround
                bottom   yellow daisy
Let us be   bosom   &blackbone
                womb   &man
Let us take   each other   one-handed

Ernie says, All my muscles necessary:
sinews   stretch&bend past
workworkwork   all weekweekweek
show more of us   &our shirt sleeves
limp with sweat
snap&tap   rise&dip   &if you can feel it you know
Fat Mamma up there givin Shady Slim the
you know what about it & if you don't know what we doin
you ain't grown enough to get in

Celebrate her thighs, Ernie says.
We
Are
The
Black
Arts
Moving

Miles Davis: The Horn, The Iris, and The Sorcerer

Woo the Prince of Darkness
with voices he can hear
when love resists the darkness
of one black man's fear

> *fill us with your spirit breathless*
> *let us go*
> *brass bruises blameless*
> *let us go*

love notes hum down the middle knuckles know it when I hit
the body trembles to my lips too high these Harlem stars come
settle the city my extra sensory perception experience my hands
against your body dig our love an existential experiment

crown the Blue Prince
dance for his tears
pose on the l.p.
clean him for a year

> *Wait*
> *I waited*
> *I waited all this time*
> *To cast that spell back on you*
> *Now you're mine*
> *mine*
> *mine*

> spellbound muted nothing left
> brought you my cross-
> road and disappeared
> into the ether

fill us, breathless spirit, let us go

You Mad Brittney Griner Is Free

1. Because black
2. Because she
3. Because she black

4. Because she because she black because she wife

5. Because she because she black because she wife
because she hoop

6. Because she because she black because she wife
because she dunk because she tatted up

7. Because free because free black because wife free
because free throw because free ink because she tall

8. Because she because she light because she wife
because she net because she inked because she height
because she loc(ked) up

9. Because she because she black because she wife
because she block because she inked because she
stat(ure) because she twist because she paid

10. Because [ ] because [ ] black because [ ] wife
because [ ] post because [ ] paint because [ ] tall
because [ ] loc & key because [ ] paid because [ ] write

11. Because she because she gold because she wife because
she fly because she art because she high top because she fade
because she paid because she write because she out

12. Because she because she black because she wife because
she pass because she ink because she tall because she fade
because she paid because she write because she out because
she black

13. Because she ~~Paul, Sarah, or Marc~~ Brittney
14. Because she ~~Kamala Joe~~ is
15. Because she ~~me~~ free

Serena Williams vs Mark Knight

you drew me with my eyes closed

curved my tongue down the middle like
Sissieretta Jones and Leontyne Price

painted these knees as pine knots bent black
filled these breasts with your mother's milk

spread my brown legs under a purple tutu
to mock my grace and gracefulness and

lifted my crown of glory because naturally
I am Althea on the court again.

Baby Archie
Seventh in the line of succession to the British throne

he'd be black by now if it weren't for the island's incessant
illusion of sun we'll call him anything except accepted of the
exceptions made in the past a veiled transparency drapes seven
silks of darkness not worth mentioning only passing glances leave
his mother out of hired hands to cast her down then what will
she think of herself her baby better off heir to the throne castle
untethered they roam the world looking for kingdoms

Si, Io sono Giancarlo Giuseppe Alessandro Esposito

Bad was not my first TV show.
Indosso mia madre's Alabama smile.

Si, sono nato in Danimarca.
Mandalorian was not my first movie.
Gideon has Papa's Italian hair.

Si, bruciato su Broadway
dieci anni prima Tom and Penn in *Taps*.
A white sheet loosely covers miei ricci.

Si, I did time with Eddie. No lines—
I listened with Papa's eyes, mia madre's
mani cioccolato tucked in my pockets.

I am an ensemble of kings, not
I Soliti Sospetti. I want you
to be taken and desperately surprised.

Yes, I am Dean Big Brother Almighty.
I wouldn't be here without Ossie and Rubie,
Sam, Larry, Jasmine, Tisha, Roger, and Spike...

Aaaaah si, I know who shot Malcolm.
Non sono stato io, ma questo e problema, si?
Denzel and Angela our only solace.

I've gone digital, il capo del futuro,
a *Far Cry* from finished. It's Papa's voice
sollevamento, and Mama's killer smile.

Queen & Slim

On the surface,
all stories
                lead to change
                direction.

Only two people
in the world
                make love
                in the summer heat.

We find ourselves
where we shouldn't be:

                under the floorboard
                wearing the night air.

Is fear at every red light
and right turn

                or only when we eat
                breakfast for dinner?

I, too, can call brothers
from never seen here,

                to pull the mask off
                for good riddance.

Freedom
doesn't last long

                or maybe once
                I pull my boots on

it lasts forever.

Mass

It can't be what we're teaching. It could be
what we're not teaching. Could be the space,
lack air of, cement block walls painted cream.
Our fingers run through the grooves like icing.
Maybe it's the food, the fights and rights to eat.
My college students ask to learn the real world.
I teach this job with taxes. Lessons come from
feeling good about ourselves, hoping in the end
they'll feel good about themselves. Does it help

I plan to teach you in my sleep? I bring you up

at dinner parties, walked you to the counselor,

sat with you over plagiarism, offered us both

the chance not to climb the disciplinary ladder.

Haven't I taught you to keep your mother from

taking your covid check? My lectures on ethos

are boring. Our class is the safest place to sleep.

Students should hide under their desks, behind

computers stowed under metal frames. We learn

with weaponry scattered about. We don't teach

enough about our feelings. We learn too much.

Our losses lie in wait to figure it out themselves.

Mass shootings beget mass murder. Mass is not

Catholic here. A tome of religion enters the class.

The bindings we reach for hang us by a thread.

Here, there's a hallway and an extra wall. I hope

my children never learn about it. They've been

hiding all their lives. Been taught the futility

of silence against the body's bloody lessons.

On the Death of Chadwick Boseman

We love you. More than that,
We count you in the number
Of black men who die here.

We tried to keep you safe, prayed
Fame wouldn't take you:
Jimi. Michael. Prince. Kobe.

We cast down conspiracies,
Educated you past twenty-four
When one out of four
Go to heaven or jail.

We prayed you'd make it,
Though the cards on this table
Are stacked. Trayvon.
Ahmaud. George.

You proved yourself
Worthy of this weight,
Took death in silence,
Died with us watching.

For your legacy,
For our sons brothers fathers,
For our daughters sisters mothers.
For every prayer your life answered,

We gather.

III.

Legion: For We Are Many

The mission—aborted in the desert of memory—
uncovered a six-pack rippling in the sun, exposed
a war-torn mind to the elements. Anthony Hill was found
wandering The Heights at Chamblee, exotic and in the wrong
place; his genitals mistaken for a cross-hairs target and gun.

Neighbors called for help. They called for him,
exhausted, climbing the complex like an obstacle course:
pull-ups over balconies, low crawling through Georgia pine,
gripping for sand between his fingers. He knocked on doors
the way he used to search for children to keep safe. A cloud
of witnesses watched him crouch in the middle of the street
like a hairless cat.

Anthony Hill, no longer contained by the mundane
like clothes and apartments, could not pull back
the pop-pop-pop-pop-pop, or discern the direction of bullets
echoing hollow in the wind, or fix his own mind over matter
long enough to change the facts to fiction, the foes to friendlies.
The best drugs mixed death-by-cop with gunpowder,
stacked and packed in the barrel of his brain.

Officer Robert Olsen arrived on the scene.
March 9, 2015: *Suspect acting erratic.* Olsen did not respond,
Keep still boy, no need for static. He did not command the situation
to run off a cliff, or exorcise the demons hiding in his skull.
Olsen's methods, manic and panic, prepared him
for a new brotherhood: Honorable service
reduced to felony murder.

Blood spilled onto the blacktop,
calm and collected. Anthony Hill:
mission completed.

Memory Foam

Viscoelasticity takes some getting used to
as if the world wasn't made to be that soft.

Bones ache to be crushed, limbs stretch
against ridges of pain and stitch.

Research proved the father too reflective,
the mother too small to keep him afloat,

that nothing soft could return the child
to face a future so viscous and dense.

Count down, the cushions exploded
under impact against a steel-plated grill,

a shatter-proof windshield. The boy
from Rocket City rises to his rest.

Weep with Those Who Weep

When you see a woman kneeling low in the morning dew
don't stop your feet from moving toward her.

When you hear the clawing, gripping, tearing of blades
in concert with incoherent wailing, ask, *Are you ok?*

When she can't answer you and can't work the phone,
reach in the wet grass and touch the face that dials.

It will sound normal when you say, *I'm at swim practice
with your wife. I think something has happened.*

Wait when you hear the woman tell her husband
that their nephew was killed in a car accident.

Keep your eyes on her breathing. Make sure
she doesn't dig herself back into the earth.

The sun is shining and your kids are in the pool,
but wait. Dig into her purse and find the keys.

Hold her arm while she stumbles to the van.
Seat her grass-limp muscles in the middle row.

Turn on the air conditioning to stop the bones
from closing in her throat.

Peel the oranges she had for her kids.
Hand her slices one by one and listen.

The Other Nine
Winbush Child Abuse Case

Because Jesus forgot one leper
lying in the basement, itching
to be free from every iniquity
and a life of crime,

Mrs. Wimbush took it upon herself
to enslave her son—*Save her son,*
she insisted. Eighteen months,
pursuant to bearing him twice.

Evil took root in the details,
vined through the house like kudzu,
bloomed malignant entrails in a fist
inside his brother, small and quiet

as prayer, saved upstairs with the others.
Muted footsteps moved above
the darkness, their sins hidden
properly beneath them.

religion (n):

the good Samaritan watches
from across the street, hands

in pockets full of hearing
faith that comes by, saying

all the right words, tied up,
bound to practice suffering,

root word: capital. We lay
sick hands, deliver no one.

Trapped in the wilderness,
blood seasoned to rot, rivers

muddy over revelation. Without
one another we succumb.

Application for Angels
After Tracy K. Smith's, "The Angels"

Let me back between the curtains
in a sheer lavender sari, sequined
halter top, and the sneakers I wear
to teach freshman comp.

She's had a hard day being a poet
in the third grade: naked, touched,
burned around the edges, a leaf
murmuring on the sidewalk.

I'll be in the door panel, undulating
purple in the mirror, quelling her
hand on the fifth, fourth, third lock
until she only needs to hear it once.

Silence is what I know: how to be
quiet with my eyes open.

The Cost of Living

It takes half the day
for a woman to bathe
her husband. The price

of life is precarious as
a footstep, how tight
we lock arms.

It requires—living
more than a moment—
energy, motion, breath.

Everything has gone up.
A week of groceries
costs three hundred dollars.

The balance can be paid
per item or shots fired
in the parking lot.

Atlantic Station charged
the death or incarceration—
without distinction—

of one twelve-year-old,
two fifteen-year-olds,
and one sixteen-year-old.

The fair market value
of one Black woman is
one Russian arms dealer.

For what will it profit a man,
if he gains the whole world,
and loses his own soul?

We risked our lives to find
Jesus. He never left us, but
leaving cost us friends.

The cost of living is
losing what we think
we'd die for.

No Better

After Tiana Clark's, "The Spot in Antioch,"
after Gwendolyn Brooks', "The Lovers of the Poor"

It was early spring and colder
than it should have been.
I was told:

> *Bring flowers.*
> *She's such a lovely mother.*

In the house, an overnight chill
loitered down a dark hallway.
The boys had gone to school.

> *She has the voice of an angel!*
> *Fills the sanctuary! Her husband*
> *does so much here in the church.*

I patted the pain around her furniture.
She absorbed the sorrow of my warmth.
Maybe it was the other way around.

> *See how they're doing...*

Something showed me the refrigerator,
the dirty dishes—not a sin—except
the water wasn't hot.

> [We stared out the window:
> Two mothers of the poor
> standing on a tight rope tethered
> to what we thought about God.]

And before I could

> *Ask about...*

A man hopped out a white truck,
lifted the steel lid of the water valve,
and shut it off.

Exodus, or How We Left Our Church of Fifteen Years

or how we stayed after so many families left
or you know folks used to call it a cult
or why does pastor call folks out like that
or Ananias & Saphira: It was their fault
or *scandaliso*—the spirit of offense
or Jezebel, because the wife
or are you hearing from God
or as long as you're hearing from the Holy Spirit
or Sarah, God hasn't said anything to me yet
or wilderness, are we going to be here forever

or that church life every Sunday Wednesday
children's church usher greeter bookstore altar
corporate prayer worship Easter pastor's birthday
pastor's wife's birthday Christmas New Year's Eve

or *baptismos*—our whole lives almost
or Pentecost, sometimes the roof would blow off
or a man walked out of his wheelchair
or a man walked out on his wife
or there's still something in the Word
or Edith, maybe it's his wife
or Moses, maybe he's just getting old
or that ministry saved us
or we were saved in that ministry
or we'd do anything but die

Unreliable Narrator

Time denies it ever happened.
Sleepwalks taking down portraits in the hall.
Taps me out to tell me I never faced perpetual night
in a hand-painted sky.

Morning recites The Law like new mercies:
There is a [   ] for this and a [   ] for that.
Makes a long story short. Colonizes my experience
with colloquialisms like *hurt people hurt people*.

Now fifteen years is two words worth nothing
but tears burned in the carpet. God's own breath
wiped soft my brow, renovated the room.

I start where my spirit won't live
without the first, without the last
name written in gold.

Blood Covenant

We left our church of fifteen years, had seen
Too much, our Noah naked as a man,
There where God had paved our paths clean
Anointed, baptized, prayer-tongued, born again.
One by one we watched the families leave,
Our loyalties and broken hearts conflicted.
What the hell is happening, Lord? our plea,
Alone, it seemed, in wilderness, convicted.
So long we'd tried to put out blazing fires,
As pain ignited embers underneath.
Like forced evacuation, we aspired
To pray for grace and wisdom as we flee.
We left our church of fifteen years and found
Our crosses whole and lifted off the ground.

IV.

To Function or Operate Properly

What if we worked on it,
took it apart,
dismantled it
in the living room
in front of the kids.
What a mess
we would make

of the wheels falling off,
rolling down the stairs,
out the door,
into the street,
past the chorus of foxgloves
heralding, trumpeting,
screaming, shouting heart
failure in a pattern of teardrops.

What tools we would use
against the machine yesterday
rusted over, caking our palms
bloody, metal to the bone.

What of our home?

These are the rules on your weekend home from the
　　　psych ward:

1. i don't\understand
　　　how you can be\sad
　　　　　for more than one\day

2. back then was simple
no one seemed to hear me\\
　　　screaming

3. my best friend found out\
i am\black

4. that guy only wanted me\for blood
dripping down the hall
　　　head against the mirror\\
　　　　　whites of his eyes sugaring the dark

5. for a while i\locked\my\doors\a lot

6. how poor was i\then
how poor am i\still
　　　i give you all\i have

7. nothing\but space
to shatter you\\
　　　princess of the tiny box we share

here\where i have the answers for your rage

I Heard The Glass Breaking.

What should have been clear
penetrates. What silk-woven
gauze spread thin, eardrum
crackle deafness. I see
the phone discordant.

She called to tell me
allow clear passage of glass,
all that glass grating, light scattered
elemental, night sand numbered;
I heard the crystal evidence.

The Man in Our Family Portrait
John Whipple Adams and his subjects, 1845

Claimed he was an artist.
A twitching black beard rendition
of Abraham Lincoln,
subtly suggesting:
Have a seat.

I could feel him posing,
the corner of the room off angle.
We would be prayer angels;
he would be god.

Eyelashes fell to a hush.
Blamelessness billowed open
to ill-advising. A handkerchief
caught mid-clutch. Poised,
persuaded. Silence steadied my knees,
my soul covered to dust the floor.

His hand rested, swearing
an oath we wouldn't remember.

The Spare Bedroom

What does it feel like behind that door
in that nosebleed section of the house?
No matter how small the hidden space,
we fill its quiet corners with fake ferns
and peace lilies, a lonely Aloe Vera.

We say we need an extra room
to keep the next guest in a plush bed
of shiny sheets and sham comforters,
with two formica tables, and a wall clock
permanently saving time.

Here is the door we pass by and peek in,
toss old furniture, lightbulbs, and pens,
the door for future guests to pass through
to the afterlife, waiting for memories
to live and die over the weekend.

Inside, that one window looks nowhere,
draped lightly like a mosquito net,
a corner view obscure, a fortress secure,
a mausoleum for one dead fly in the sill,
lifeless, except dust mites bathing in sunlight.

Sheltered out of the elements,
captive like mice in the wall, we tiptoe,
listen for the thinness. Light creeps in,
touching the feet of passersby as if to ask,
who will stay and when?

Treating Sarge and Betty to Ice Cream

Sometimes they can't hear
you against so many

other words they heard before.
Repetition is an angry thing.

Sometimes they remember you
better than you were,

better than them. Memory
is a kid in a candy store.

They have no time
to trifle with little

things like longsuffering.
Patience is a gift unwrapped

by grooms and new moms.
Sometimes they don't say

what you wished.
They say what they mean.

Niceties are for knickknacks
and funerals and conversation

is an overdressed picnic guest.
So talk above the fan blowing

history in their ears.
Remember they were better

than they think they were.
Give them time

with their little things,
which is you.

Say the words they wished.
Say what you mean. Repeat it.

Save niceties
for knickknacks and funerals.

Mittraphap Road

Fluid destinations,
home locations,
and occupations.
Never too far,
in a way,
we always know
exactly where we are.

When your goals
were north in Nong Khai
and my morals
were south in Saraburi.

Foot and carriage,
hoof and yoke,
packed solid the earth
so long beneath us.
For one day

we would say,
it was worth the time,
distance, calls,
cards and pictures.

We would stop playing
games, rising and falling over
Yen Mountains of marriages,
babies, and too much time away.

Smoother, now
paved six lanes wide,
proud, expanded
by asphalt and cement
to outlast us.

Burn The Whole Thing

inside out; buy ancient roots online.
Exercise and Vitamin D will help.
Meanwhile, I set an appointment

for the doctor to confirm the long
dry spells my body has reported.
It will take distance, years maybe,

to drive through this country town
with one red light: no one knows
when I entered or when I'll leave.

Days circle black around my eyes,
drawing what little iron I have left.
Night bursts lightning, poured-out

sweat, wet everywhere except where
he wants me, because time pulls
my womb like a ship out at sea.

Moon Rising

It spends the day waiting under water:
beneath the edge
the other side.

It measures out the deep, perhaps.
Fathoms to climb
breaks the surface.

Then shadows night like a ghost ship.
Its entrance veiled
and catching fire.

Sky burns black silk the atmosphere.
Slow to invade
the moon appears.

Stars bow and fade.
Light casts a path
to midnight sea.

The Ocean

shouldn't embrace the night.
Planting, growing shadows
in a blue house mirage. Joining,
plotting elements to gather and throw.
Thirsting, tempting, death by excursion.

shouldn't play Marco Polo.
Pitching baby lights across
a pale playground. Charming,
luring like line pulling
tight into it. Lifting,
shifting directions
as if lost.

shouldn't be buoyant.
No, it shouldn't be true,
balanced or endless. Soaking,
beaming flecks skin deep. Casting
back into the black, broken,
a trail of edges.

It shouldn't be touching
the sky like that.

The First Sunday Morning in November

Purple leaves paste to the ground like papier-mâché.
Gravity pulls the browning grass back to the earth
with invisible stillness so powerful nothing moves.

Even the trees hide death in plain sight. Tiny stems
hang tethered in time. The West Wind patiently subsides
in the tilt of a burning leaf. No need to rush.

What do the children know about November,
the harvest moon, the silent stars, the birth and death
of a landscape holding its breath yellow?

I will let them rise to their own conclusions
about a sky that only hints enough light for the day,
how to sleep at night only and shine without the sun.

Winter in Georgia

1.
First, the snow gently falls,
melts on top the standing blades of grass
and sounds like dew the sky—silent—calls.

With all the snow of future, present, past,
and all the snow Almighty has in store,
heaven knows how long the storm will last.

With noses pressed, we watch for more.
Our expectation rises white and round
until at last, we tumble out the door.

The mailbox, fence, and bushes all around
covered in wet packable snow
to aim in jest at enemies newly found.

2.
Bitter winds whip and rack the window pane,
a winter song with lyrics icy and profane.
Inside we huddle, wrapped in our domain.

Snow piles on the fence as frosty cones,
brittle branches bend and snap like bones,
inside fire beats the wind and moans.

All white, all still, all frozen—we wish—like time,
to see it all at once, the snow world shine.
Ah, but we are warm, like fire divine.

3.
While winter still, I wonder
when spring will rise with fonder
colors where we'll wander
outdoors to breathe and play.

While cozy sleep and slumber
calls all to blankets under,
we wait the cold, cold tundra
to melt in spring's new day.

A long, long wait we're waiting,
feign patience, though it's baiting
this season's slow march grating
so halts our busy way.

But hear the North Wind laughing
with each storm cloud amassing
blows ice and snow in passing
and holds our door at bay.

V.

Rain on a September Morning

It's early and it's been raining for hours.
The dog sniffs the door and whimpers.
No one wakes up. No one will walk him.

This poem has been raining in me
For days, weeks, maybe even months.
I love laughing, but I'm just as likely
To side-eye, *What's with all the rain?*

I'm all trauma and long memory, gaps
Between rain drops, the blue dot on radar
Watching green yellow orange red,
All the colors of rain come my way.

What kind of poet are you? a mentor asked.
Since then, I have been sitting upright
Waiting for the rain to tell me.

I'm the black rain experience, a late bloomer
Hiding beside a basket of clothes, rubbing
Nacho's backside with my foot.

Studying for the exams has taught me
More about rain than I wanted to know.
It's romantic how God made me
To notice the trees and rain.

Where would I be without stanzas to enter
And leave in the rain? Each line is a little couch
Where a few words sit next to each other
Wondering what will happen when their knees touch.

I spent the last two months without
A woman on my study schedule.
Everything I know about black poets I have
Taught myself between thunder and light.

This is how I come in from the rain:
I close my eyes and imagine
I'm manageable.

Special Thanks

I thank God. Without Him, none of this would be possible.

I acknowledge that the lands on which I pursued my graduate studies were once inhabited by indigenous nations and were cultivated by the enslavement of my African ancestors.

Many thanks to the Sewanee Writers Conference, the Hambidge Center, and my cohorts at Kennesaw State University and Georgia State University: Leata Thomas Selby, Molly Lathem, Kristen Ruiz, Allison Bennett, Nancy Anderson, Sugar LaFae, Caroline Crew, Anna Sandy Elrod, Greg Emilio, Scarlet Peterson, Emily Lake Hansen, Ashe Prevett, Cat Chitwood, Mike Saye, Tarfia Faizullah, George Abraham, Dustin Pearson, and Tiana Clark.

Tremendous thanks to Carl Phillips, Beth Gylys, Jenny Sadre-Orafai, Ralph Wilson, Anthony Grooms, Lara Smith-Sitton, John Holman, Andrea Jurjevic, David Bottoms (resting in peace), Megan Sexton, Josh Russell, Lynee Gaillet, Sherri Joseph, Sharan Strange, Chris Martin, Jesse Graves, and Alice Friman.

Special thanks to my extended family, those with whom I've broken bread, shared laughter, shed tears, and prayed.

I thank my parents Charles and Carrie Salter whose great sacrifices provided Lynn, John-Charles, and me with knowledge, wisdom, creativity, and every attainable opportunity.

To my husband Akil, and to my amazing children Nathaniel and Maxine. This love is for you.

About the Author

Photo by BJB Glamour Photography

Valerie A. Smith has a PhD in Poetry from Georgia State University and an MA in Professional Writing from Kennesaw State University, where she is a Lecturer of English. A 2022 Sewanee Writers Conference Scholar and Hambidge Center Fellow, her poems appear in *The South Carolina Review, Aunt Chloe, Weber—The Contemporary West, Spectrum, Obsidian, Crosswinds, Dogwood, Solstice, Oyster River Pages, Wayne Literary Review*, and elsewhere. Find her online at www.valeriesmithwriter.com.

Other Sundress Titles

Ruin & Want
José Angel Araguz
$20.00

Nocturne in Joy
Tatiana Johnson-Boria
$12.99

Age of Forgiveness
Caleb Curtiss
$12.99

Another Word for Hunger
Heather Bartlett
$12.99

Little Houses
Athena Nassar
$16.00

Where My Umbilical is Buried
Amanda Galvan Huynh
$12.99

In Stories We Thunder
V. Ruiz
$12.99

the Colored page
Matthew E. Henry
$12.99

Slack Tongue City
Mackenzie Berry
$12.99

Year of the Unicorn Kidz
jason b. crawford
$12.99

Sweetbitter
Stacey Balkun
$12.99

Something Dark to Shine In
Inès Pujos
$12.99

www.ingramcontent.com/pod-product-compliance
Lightning Source LLC
Chambersburg PA
CBHW031149090426
42738CB00008B/1275